# COPING WITH INNER-TURMOIL

## BY CHERRY SCOTT

**CHERRY ENTERPRISES**

\*

# COPING WITH INNER-TURMOIL

This book "Coping With Inner-Turmoil" and author's first book, "A Black Woman Speaks" may be purchased for educational, business, or sales promotion use. For information, please call or write: Special Markets Dept. Cherry Enterprises, 200 Riverfront Park, Suite 1105 Detroit, MI 48226, Telephone: (313) 393-5929

## FOREWORD

COPING WITH INNER-TURMOIL was written to aid in the the elimination of the negative emotions anger, bitterness, resentment, loneliness and the agony of defeat.

As we all strive to obtain for ourselves quality living standards, we sometimes find ourselves in the grip of negative feelings that keep us from having the types of positive attitudes that establish and maintain positive actions in our lives as we function in the home, at work, at school and at play.

COPING WITH INNER-TURMOIL was written to aid in the establishment and maintenance of more positive relationships with others as we all strive to obtain for ourselves maximum peace, equality, prosperity and ultimately successful living.

## *COPING   WITH   INNER-TURMOIL*

COPING WITH:

                                        PAGE

Anger........................................................................1

Bitterness.................................................................10

Resentment.............................................................15

Loneliness...............................................................24

Defeat......................................................................31

Moving Forward and Upward
Toward Inner-Peace, Success
and Greatness...........................................................37

## <u>COPING WITH ANGER</u>

From infancy to the last days of our lives, most of us will likely have to cope with anger, as life will not always present itself as we would like it to. From our parents, to our friends, our children, lovers, associates and foes, something in these relationships may cause us to "blow up" in anger. Oftentimes, out of anger, we do more harm to ourselves than to the objects of our anger. Thus, it becomes a necessity of life that we learn to "cope" with our anger, in a positive way, controlling our tempers. For, far too many people have destroyed their families, careers, friendships, the lives of others and even themselves as a result of an inability to"cope" with anger in a positive way.

But before anyone can "cope" with something, one must first define it, to understand it, to cope with it. By definition "anger is a revengeful passion or emotion directed against one who inflicts a real or supposed

1

wrong. Anger is an emotion. Anger is a feeling that any human being can experience on any given day or moment in time. Since it is known that feelings can most often be controlled, anger can seemingly be no big deal. But anger is a big deal because more and more, we are not controlling our feelings...our anger.

Because we are not controlling our feelings, coping with anger in a positive way, anger is often turning into tragedy. Our inability to "cope" with anger is evidenced by the countless acts of violence against spouses, relatives, friends and mere acquaintances, committed by people overcome with anger. Feelings of anger, if uncontrolled, can turn to rage, of violent intensity, much like the force of a raging storm-- overwhelming and destructive.

Rage is the result of anger when one does not know how or has not been taught to control one's own feelings. So how does one cope with anger in an effort to maintain peace, dignity and respect in our dealings with one another?

Considering how intensely competitive we have become, most of us would like to think of ourselves as civilized human beings, willing to give the respect and treatment of others that we expect. But with negativity running rampant, it often becomes difficult in the face of pain, unfairness, disrespect, alienation and depravation to go about our daily living without hurting someone, simply because we ourselves feel hurt and angry. Unable to cope with our anger, we lash out at others to transfer the pain and anger we feel about our own lives.

When we lash out at others in our inability to cope with our own anger, we create vicious cycles of anger being, transferred back and forth in our relationships. By contrast, we must learn to cope with our anger to eliminate it from our lives. For as we transfer our anger to others it eventually comes right back to us, often with greater force and velocity.

This is not what we want. I am sure we all would like to live our lives as free of anger as possible. So how do we cope with anger in a positive way to eliminate it from our lives? How does a person "cope" with anger as an individual in his or her own personal life.

To cope with anger in a positive way, one must first establish a personal commitment of remaining calm any time one may have a tendency to become angry-- losing control. Acknowledgment of the things that make you angry during moments of joy can aid in coping with anger in a positive way. As you become experienced in life, you will become aware of the things that people do to anger, frustrate or disrespect you. Knowing and accepting that some people, as a result of their personal problems, will intentionally set out to cause you pain will help in "coping" with the anger that mean-spirited people might try to cause you. Accepting that some people are "troubled," as a result of their own personal pains, try not to take all malicious actions personally. View unkind individuals as sick and in need of care. Try not to let mean and vicious people anger you. Steer clear of them as much as possible until they get better. But should these type people lash out at you in attempts to anger you, knowing they are sick should enable you to ignore them and their actions--not getting angry. In time you will come to know the ways that people express and vent their emotional pains. With this you will come to sympathize with mean-spirited individuals, as opposed to becoming angry by their negative words or actions against you.

Realize that it will take time, practice and patience to develop the skills of "coping" with anger in a positive way. Reflecting on your contacts with others, you can most likely realize that anger is an emotion that often builds on itself. In tiny portions, annoyances too small to acknowledge build on themselves turning to anger. Catching some of us off guard, minor feelings of discomfort, can quickly turn to anger, overwhelming us. A key to "coping" with anger in a positive way is to defuse emotional discomfort <u>before</u> it turns to anger. A significant way of defusing an anger causing situation is to remove yourself from the environment that seems bound to cause you emotional stress, pain or discomfort.

But should a situation catch you off guard causing emotions of anger to suddenly influence your actions, condition yourself to quickly take a deep breath in an effort to reduce the stress and tension in your body that usually accompanies anger. Relax your body, whether standing or sitting. Say to yourself, "I can handle this anger causing situation calmly and rationally." "I refuse to let the actions of anyone control my emotions and behavior." Quiet calm is a significant step in the right direction toward "coping" with anger in a positive way. To turn an uncomfortable moment around, physically or mentally remove yourself from the situation. Tune out everything and everyone around you. Think of a beautiful body of water, a love interest, a favorite experience, achievement or aspiration. Whatever visions of joy you prefer, learn to submerge yourself within thoughts of peace and happiness whenever instances of anger threaten to overtake your actions or behavior in a negative way. Totally remove your thoughts from the volcanic type eruptions that are sure to arise from angry feelings, angry words and angry deeds.

It should be an ultimate goal to avoid negative situations, circumstances, relationships, encounters and reactions. But when negativity must be dealt with, it is best to deal with negative forces or circumstances in a manner that is socially acceptable to establish and maintain the dignity and respect that you and everyone deserves in life. It is important that you project the message that you expect to be treated with respect and fairness. When necessary, to maintain respect in your relationships, say what has to be said to make others aware of uncomfortable or disrespectful treatment and let the matter go. Discuss any matters of wrongful acts against you with a family member, friend, or even stranger to vent any remaining anxiety, stress, frustration, anger, bitterness or need to cry--to clear your inner-being. Refuse to carry angry emotions around as emotional baggage.

Go forward in life with a positive, calm attitude and mindset that peace, happiness, respect and satisfaction are the rights of all. Realize that whatever anger causing dilemma you faced moments or days ago, that the incident is just a tiny spec in the picture you paint call "life." The brush is yours to paint the picture of your life dreams. Don't allow your strokes in life to be controlled by anger, vengeance or malice.

Go forward and upward, viewing anger as an insect to small to deal with.

SIDESTEP ANGER AND CROSS OVER TO SUCCESS!!!

# # # # # # #

## <u>COPING WITH BITTERNESS</u>

Bitterness is the state, the emotion, the attitude that becomes a part of you when you stay angry a little too long.   Bitterness is the poison that invades your life when the emotional pain from an act against you won't seem to go away.

Bitterness is the ever-present cloud over your head that rains down in your heart and mind, causing your life to seem stormy and dark...sometimes for no apparent reason.   Bitterness is the anger you befriend that acts as an agitator, keeping your attitude and emotions tense, filled with stress, anger and pain. Bitterness can be your worst enemy as it stands by your side, follows your around, even leading you deeper into a forest of pain, frustration, confusion, threatening to destroy your family, career and even your dreams. Bitterness can steer you away from the opportunities and success that you really seek in life.

Regardless of all the conditioning and training that we receive to control our anger, occasionally we find ourselves holding on to anger as if it were a long lost love or favorite teddy bear. Because of acts against us, or disappointment in our lives, anger may seem to be a safe haven for the pain we feel. The positive difference in "coping" with the anger, is to release it, not allowing anger to turn to bitterness.

Knowing the power of hurt, pain and disappointment, it is not always easy to forget and release the thoughts and emotions that cause bitterness. But just like all other negative emotions, bitterness as well, must be controlled by you. Controlling your negative emotions is "coping" with internal feelings in an effort to not be controlled by negative forces in your heart and mind. Coping with bitterness is your ability to rid yourself of negative emotions that are the friends of frustration, stagnation, heartache and pain.

To rid yourself of bitter feelings is to, in a sense, forgive and forget. Forgiving and forgetting a wrong against you does not necessarily mean that you are "weak." Learn from painful incidents against you to prevent the same types of wrongs in the future. Wrongful acts or incidents against you should be used to build your own personal storehouse of wisdom, cautioning you against possible danger zones in life. Don't allow yourself to hold grudges against others, systems or institutions. Take anger causing situations in stride, vowing "not" to be pulled down by the bitterness that is sure to follow if you choose to embrace and marry your anger.

Thoughts of new and better days ahead to reap the rewards of your dreams is a positive way of "coping" with the onset of bitterness. Think of life as yours alone...your special gift...to live as you please with no limitations, no boundaries, no problems or people to stand in your way. Move forward with the thought that, though the roads you choose in life may be rocky or come to a dead end when least expected, there is always a way around, over or under any life obstacle. Refuse to get stuck behind a wall of your own bitterness.

When others influence bitter feelings in your heart, realize that they too have lives to live in the best way that they know how. And oftentimes, it is not that others *intentionally* seek to cause you harm or pain. Sometimes we cause pain, anger and bitterness in others as a result of our own selfishness, insecurities, pain and perhaps reckless attempts to secure happiness and success for ourselves.

So do not hold on to your anger to become bitterness when life seems hard and unfair. With positive thoughts of the future, build a life of abundant, peace, happiness and prosperity for yourself and those you love and care about. Say good-bye to bitterness today!

GO FORWARD IN PEACE AND FORGIVENESS!

# **COPING WITH RESENTMENT**

Resentment is another emotion, a feeling that often clouds our vision as we proceed down our roads to success, happiness and prosperity. By definition, resentment is *a feeling of displeasure at something regarded as an injury or insult.*

But just as most negativity has increased in the nineties, resentment as well has grown to resemble a stronger force and barrier than it's dictionary definition. Unfortunately, we now resent one another when there has been no obvious injury or insult. Some of us have grown to resent others simply because of their presence alone. We resent others, often, when we feel that our own sense of security is threatened. Thus, many of us may cause resentful feelings in others, just as we ourselves feel resentful towards others. Resentment becomes a serious problem, threatening the well-being of ourselves and others, as resentment exists as yet another emotional barrier against open communication, social harmony, educational growth, personal growth, understanding and personal awareness.

Resentment is especially troublesome as some of us can become victims of resentment without even realizing it. In some cases we may simply present ourselves in such a way that may come across as offensive, arrogant, condescending, patronizing or simply vain, causing resentment in others. When emotional discomfort in relationships exist, we soon realize that something is wrong. A relationship seems unjustifiably tense and forced.

Hence, we often wonder "why" certain relationships seem uncomfortable, unfriendly and even at times, stressful. When barriers seem obvious, in what should be, at least workable, impersonal relationships, resentment is often the cause. It becomes clearer that resentment is the cause of most seemingly strained relationships as we begin to give or receive discourteous or less than gracious treatment. It is sad to see in far too many instances, we resent others for reasons outside or beyond a person's control.

We resent others because of race and other physical attributes, i.e. skin color, hair, height, weight etc. Making matters worse, we resent others for accomplishments, social status and a host of other things that we deem injurious to our own grandiose, mental perceptions of ourselves. Having our own ideas of who we think we think we are and what we represents, resentment, creeps in when we feel over-shadowed by others. Our feelings of inadequacy are thus blamed on others, causing resentment and disharmony in our relationships.

To be true to our own maximum potentials, we must come to realize that if we take a close look at ourselves, we will realize that the resentful feelings that we often feel toward others are in fact longings to possess the characteristics or qualities that we see in others. The first step to "coping" with resentment in a positive way is to realize that "resentment" is a negative emotion that must be controlled, if not eliminated as a part of who you are, how you feel, act and react to people. Feelings of resentment block our abilities to function with open minds and healthy, positive, optimistic attitudes toward what we really want out of life for ourselves. But of course, we can not always control an instant and spontaneous thought, even those of resentment. Thus another key to increased inner-peace is to "cope" with your feelings of resentment in a positive way.

"Coping" with your feelings of resentment in a positive way will aid in your own effort to genuinely feel good about yourself. Because as you may come to know, feelings of resentment become obvious, especially to the person you resent when left unchecked and uncontrolled. When you allow your feelings of resentment to overwhelm you, you present yourself as an insecure, frustrated individual. Worse over, you present yourself as a person with low-self esteem. For as you set out to alienate, aggravate or infuriate the person you resent, you actually complement and flatter this person, especially if this person has done nothing to insult or injure you. In essence, an obvious display of resentment towards others, is an outward plea for sympathy as you struggle with your feelings of insecurity, inadequacy and possibly inferiority.

To cope with feelings of resentment in a positive way, is to confront yourself with "the truth" about how you feel about yourself, relative or compared to others. To cope with feelings of resentment, to eliminate them, mentally and emotionally, charge into the face of that which you resent. Force yourself to embrace the symbol of your resentment. Dissect the characteristics of your resentment, to define it, to understand it, to overcome what it is about the object of your resentment that makes you frustrated or even angry. If honest with yourself, you may come to realize that you view the person or object of your resentment as superior to who or what you are. Feeling that another person is superior to you is a problem that you establish and maintain in your own mind. Thus feelings of inferiority can only be eliminated by the establishment and maintenance of your own "increased" self-worth and value.

However if you are resentful of the way a person treats you, seek out a rational and non-combative way of letting the person know how you feel. With patience, understanding and open communication, two intelligent people should be able to work through the difficulties that hinder harmonious and workable relationships.

However, if you are the culprit in harboring resentful feelings toward someone who simply makes you feel less wonderful, less intelligent, less beautiful or less anything, you do more harm to yourself by blatantly exhibiting feelings of resentment. By your negative, resentful behavior, you compliment and flatter the objects of your resentment in that most people come to realize when they are disliked simply because someone sees them as superior or more privileged in some way. Hence, in your resentment, you boost the self-esteem and confidence of the object of your resentment confirming their self-worth and value as you de-value your own. Thus it is in your own best interest to establish and maintain positive ways of "coping" with your resentment.

Coping with your resentment in a positive way means coming to the realization that the object of your resentment is the the cause of the negative feelings that you may feel inside. To be fair to your own potential for success, realize that feelings of inadequacy, insecurity and even inferiority have nothing to do with other people, things, circumstances or situations. If things outside yourself make you feel less than good about yourself, realize that people or situations are not superior to you... they are simply different.

To change how you feel about people, circumstances, or situations toward a more positive vain...change yourself. Improve the way you look! Improve the way you present yourself! Change the way you act and react to the activities of your life. Raise your educational level. Make more money. If resentment seems to be a constant problem for you, commit to becoming a better person--on an ongoing basis. Refuse to dwell on what others have that you do not.

Find your joy in getting all the peace, love, happiness and prosperity out of life that you can. Share these treasures of life that you obtain and you will have no time or energy for resentment in your life, heart, mind or soul. To eliminate "resentment" as a reaction to people, places, or things, refuse to spend your time and energy on negative thoughts.

The opportunities of success, wealth, happiness and more are everywhere for the taking. If opportunities do not come or do not readily present themselves to you, CREATE YOUR OWN OPPORTUNITIES FOR ALL THAT YOU DESIRE AND DESERVE IN LIFE.

Get your fair share of all that life has to offer...or someone else will! Just remember that there is a storehouse of opportunity with your name alone on it. There is no value in seeing life through eyes of resentment.

Exchange your thoughts of resentment for thoughts of self- fulfillment, personal growth and success!!!!!!!!!!!!!!

## <u>COPING WITH LONELINESS</u>

*loneliness...far too often chases us into the arms of self-destruction*

Though most of us would like to think of ourselves as strong and capable, more than a few of us experiences loneliness as an overwhelming and tragic circumstance. Thus, we often run, with reckless abandon into the arms of whomever or whatever will have us. Fearing disconnection from anything or everything, we often find ourselves embraced in the arms of unhealthy relationships, defeat, mediocrity, frustration, bitterness, crime, poverty, drug addiction, and even self-destruction.

With all that society has accomplished, with all of its opportunities, we now find ourselves overwhelmed by choices, blinding us to what most of us truly seek from life...love, happiness, peace of mind and prosperity. With every divorce, rape, murder, suicide and all other tragedies against us, we find ourselves asking "why" and how" such human tragedy can be taking place in a society so civilized, so technologically advanced and brimming with opportunity and potential.

Though answers abound, not many point to "loneliness"as a contributing factor to the tragedies of broken homes, broken dreams, abuse, violence and destruction in American cities, communities and homes. But if we could force ourselves to capture quiet moments from our busy schedules, most would realize that loneliness--a state of being without sympathetic companionship, can be a tragically depressing time for a person who cannot "cope" with being alone.

Hence, we frantically run in fear, from loneliness...in essence from ourselves. Avoiding loneliness, we often connect ourselves with people, things and circumstances, that are sometimes negative, detrimental and even destructive to our well-being, safety or security.

And as we run from the negative feelings of loneliness, the companions we choose are too often band-aid fixes for a more serious problem. The problem being, our inability to "cope" with loneliness in a positive way. Being alone does not always mean that one is lonely. Some people are fortunate enough to enjoy times of aloneness just as much as time spent with people with whom they may work or play. Being alone becomes loneliness when a prolonged, depressing desire to connect with someone or something is not met. The state of loneliness becomes a tragedy for some of us as self-destruction and self-inflicted pain, are willing and always ready companions for a person overly afraid of being alone with one's self and the biting truth of who we really are. Yes, taking the time to acknowledge and work toward creating and maintaining what is best for you can be hard work. It must be realized that life is a balancing act and in order for us to feel the type of satisfaction and inner-peace that we seek, we must work hard to keep all aspects of what is important to us at acceptable and satisfying levels.

Marriage and family, finances, health and physical fitness, social contacts, emotional peace, and mental growth are some of the basic needs of most people. Spending time alone allows us to take personal stock of what areas in our lives are weak and which areas our are strong. As we run from aloneness, our lives can become unbalanced, causing pain and anguish in all other parts of our lives. (As *I* was never directly/effectively made aware of the importance of marriage and family, as an adult, this area is significantly unbalanced relative to all other areas of my life, causing pain and anguish. Thus I do not always realize my own perceived maximum potentials, having to put forth extra strength in "coping with loneliness in a positive way.") So, comes the question, "how does one "cope" with loneliness or being alone against one's wishes in a positive way?"

To cope with loneliness in a positive way, realize that spending time alone does not *have* to be a bad experience or negative state. Being alone is a state that we can change at any given moment. The difference between positive and negative results (in coping with loneliness) lie in the choices we make in exchange for our loneliness. When we choose quick and easy fixes to alleviate loneliness, we often find ourselves more troubled with our chosen companions than in our states of being alone.

Thus it is important to condition yourself to make the time you spend alone positive experiences. Use the time you spend alone to become one of your own best friends and support system. Get to know yourself, to like yourself, to love yourself--to improve and increase the love you have to give and share with others--decreasing loneliness in your life.

When alone, don't waste time dwelling on thoughts of what you could be doing with others. Quality companionship will come to you as you determine the type of companionship that is best for you. In turn, when you unite yourself with people and activities that provide the type of quality social contact you seek, you will find increased enjoyment in that you will have earned the time to give to others because you have first given your own life quality time, consideration and concern.

In your time alone, strive to walk away from aloneness a better person in at least one way, if not many. In times alone get some much needed rest. Pamper yourself, relaxing yourself--mind body and soul. Take time spent alone to rid your mind, body and spirit of all that is unclean, unhealthy and emotionally painful or stressful.

With a fresh and rested mind, increase your intelligence. Always have a book close at hand to learn at least one new thing about better health, better living, finance, your past, your present circumstances, your future. Set a short or long range goal each and every day. End each day of your life with the thought that you are a better person than you were the day before! Forgive yourself and others for shortcomings and flaws. At the end of each day, vow to be a better person tomorrow than you were today! BEING ALONE IS A PERSONAL TIME FOR REJUVENATION!

## **COPING WITH DEFEAT**

Defeat--"The failure to win--losing." Such a common, simple word. Yet some of us experience "defeat" *the act or state of losing* as a complex, catastrophic, disastrous and destructive state. Yes, defeat can be an overwhelmingly negative experience for those of us who have not learned to "cope" with defeat in a positive way.

Evidence of a person unable to "cope" with defeat or a setback in a positive way shows itself in a lack of personal-life growth, enthusiasm to try new things and a reluctance to set and reach on-going life goals. A person unable to cope with defeat in a positive way becomes comfortable with his or her life as it is--even if that life becomes unsatisfying and destructive. A person unable to "cope" with defeat in a positive way often becomes almost terrified of defeat, opting to apprehensively go through life never knowing the rewards and beauty of living a well-balanced life to the fullest.

As many of us grapple with the trials and tribulations of succeeding in the nineties and beyond, a great number of us bond with mediocrity and less as we succumb to the fears, anguish and pain that can accompany a moment of defeat, an unfulfilled dream, a perceived and lost "chance of a lifetime." What we must learn to do if we are to turn our dreams to reality is to learn how and maintain a vigilant ability to "cope" with defeat in a positive way--always reaching, always striving, always growing to fully enjoy the gift called "life."

To "cope" with defeat in a positive way is to view the act or state of losing as a learning experience. To experience defeat with a positive and healthy attitude is to realize that defeat is a process, a step, an event along your life journey to a satisfying and fulfilling state of being. This is to say, that a lot of us fall prey to defeat very early in our lives, not realizing that life is a very long journey, filled with opportunity, potential and the unknown. Unfortunately, some of us in our inabilities to "cope with defeat" in a positive way, get hung up on an overwhelming defeat in our teens, twenties or even our forties not realizing that life provides on-going opportunities and that we have the time and the capabilities to fulfill even our most loftiest of dreams, if only we have the courage to try.

An important key to living a fulfilling and satisfying life is to have many dreams, at many different levels. Set goals and have dreams that are easy to obtain, slightly challenging to obtain and <u>very</u> challenging to obtain. Hence you can never really lose in life because you are always winning at something-- though not all things. As you win and lose in life, build for yourself strength reserves to aid in handling future adversities and defeats...which are sure to come as we can not always control the outcome of life situations, no matter how diligently we plan, prepare or even work.

Become aware of the effect that "losing" has on you and how certain losses impact your life. Determining what is important to you in living a well-balanced and satisfying life, will help you to realize that it is not important to win at all things. More significantly, knowing what is important to you should determine how you spend your life energies to reduce the losses in areas of your life that are most important to your continued well-being. If financial security, marriage and family is important to you, then these are the things that you should learn about, establish and maintain in your life for successful living.

To avoid feeling like "a loser" in life never devote vast amounts of your energies, time and effort to things that are not important to you. Many people learn too late in life that significant attention to things unimportant to them can result in devastation and destructive frustration when they find themselves unable to satisfy their own basic needs and desires.

Determine as early in life as possible the things that will make you most proud of yourself, bringing you the greatest joys, rendering you a responsible and respectable person. The things that make you feel the best about who you are and what you stand for are the things in which you will want to become the most skilled and knowledgeable. As you mature and grow, expose yourself to new and rewarding experiences, allowing yourself to change in positive ways to flow with the ever-changing times of society. As you become better and better at satisfying and fulfilling your life needs and desires, you will come to find that the word "defeat" has very little significance to you.

Defeat can one day come to mean simply "detour" for you. A positive way of "coping with defeat" is to know that achieving success and satisfaction in life is not an absolute, straight and narrow journey. Fortunately, in life there are many, many ways of establishing and maintaining the successes and "wins" in your life that you need to feel good about yourself and the life that you live. Know that life is not a win or lose activity. And even though your efforts may not always result in the outcome you seek today, positive coping skills provide for entirely new opportunities to win.

Always remember that in everyone's life there will be roadblocks, pitfalls, obstacles, struggle and setbacks. Constant self-improvement and personal growth in all areas of your life is key in offsetting defeat. When your life efforts are positive and abundant, occasional defeats will only serve to strengthen you, propelling you toward greatness and all the wonderful things in life that you desire, seek and deserve!

## <u>MOVING FORWARD AND UPWARD<br>TOWARD INNER-PEACE<br>SUCCESS AND GREATNESS</u>

To move forward and upward toward inner-peace, success and greatness, realize that you were given your gift of life for a purpose. Moreover, you were born with the right to enjoy your life in peace, harmony and prosperity. But you were also born to change the condition of man and womankind in only a way that you know how or will discover.

All that we are and all that life has become with all of it's technology, conveniences, pleasures and opportunities exist because of individuals just like you and me. The people of the human race that paved and continue to pave the way for modern technologies and conveniences are people who have lived life to the fullest, contributing to the continued betterment of man and womankind.

To take your place in the chain of human greatness, accept without prejudice that life is abundant with opportunity for those who embrace the life principles of self-respect, personal growth, on-going education, respect for others, creativity and productivity.

Unfortunately, so many of us fall off or are pushed from the life tracks of self-improvement, self-respect and thus satisfaction and success. Adding to the mishap of adversity, some of us never recover, from adversity, wallowing in self-pity and defeat. Inflicting ourselves with the most traumatic wound, we give in to emotional turmoil, never fulfilling dreams, purposes or any goals that will make us feel proud of who we are and the greatness that we should represent.

Most of us are basically aware of the principles and processes necessary to establish and maintain healthy, happy, peaceful, satisfying, successful and prosperous lives. Unfortunately, we often become disillusioned and frustrated as we surrender to the emotional turmoil of anger, bitterness, disappointment, resentment, guilt, loneliness and defeat.

An important factor in establishing and maintaining the type of lifestyle that you desire in life is to first accept the fact that your journey through life may not always be as smooth and straight forward as you would like it to be. Also know that everyone will come face to face with unexpected adversities or obstacles. To make your life journey a smoother and more successful one, learn to "cope" with the inner-turmoil or negative emotions that you may feel when your life-struggles seem a bit overwhelming, too frequent and unfair.

To reduce the inner-turmoil that you may feel in life, regardless of your age, sex or nation of origin, establish for yourself a vision, a destination, an accomplishment, in life that you can call your own and be proud of. To establish your vision get to know who you are. Identify your likes, dislikes, talents, interests, capabilities, strengths and weaknesses.

Knowing yourself is to know what your motivations are--what you care about in life or what is of no concern to you at all. Knowing the things--family, career, creativity, financial security--that bring you the greatest joys should establish, define and lay the foundation for your vision, your destination, purpose success and satisfaction in life. Wandering at random throughout your life with no clear direction or purpose is an almost sure way to live your life feeling unfulfilled, frustrated and victimized by your own inner-turmoil.

To mold who you are and who you want to be into a foundation of inner-strength, inner-peace and satisfying success, establish and remain true to a high sense of self-love and self-respect. Establish and maintain a strong sense of diligence, discipline and determination in creating and maintaining the peace, happiness and prosperity that you need in your life to feel good about yourself, even in comparison to others.

To successfully move forward and upward toward inner-peace, success and greatness, always be honest and fair with yourself. Feel good about your strengths, embrace them and let them spur you on to higher heights.

To paint a true life portrait of your essence and excellence, have the courage to confront and "cope" with your weaknesses to reduce them, as they may one day overwhelm you, overshadowing or destroying even your greatest strengths. And even though "common courtesy" is fast becoming uncommon, establish a "greatness" about yourself in that rudeness toward others is not considered your "power" or strength. Rudeness and disrespect toward others is a blatant display of inner-pain, turmoil and an inability to cope with one's own frustration in a positive way.

Create and present your sense of worth as a result of your positive accomplishments, talents and aspirations. Knowing how corrupt, abusive and destructive society has become as we approach the year 2000, establish yourself as a role model for young people and adults as well. Establish yourself as a person that you like and that others can find likeable and respectable.

Moving forward and upward toward inner-peace and greatness is to establish your life as a pattern to be followed and observed by others for the continued greatness of man and womankind.

As you learn to cope with inner-turmoil in a positive way, you aid in increasing the peace, happiness and prosperity in society that we all seek. As you establish and maintain your own individual greatness, you provide a ray of hope, the much needed support and the potential for greatness for all others.

Human greatness depends on you. Establish and maintain your individual greatness for your sake and mine. You and I "alike" are the keepers of the greatness of man and womankind.